this is n
entertainment
A Documentary Poem

this is no longer entertainment
A Documentary Poem

Christodoulos Makris

Dostoyevsky Wannabe Originals
An Imprint of Dostoyevsky Wannabe

First Published in 2019
by Dostoyevsky Wannabe Originals

Dostoyevsky Wannabe Originals is an imprint of Dostoyevsky Wannabe publishing.

Cover design by Dostoyevsky Wannabe
www.dostoyevskywannabe.com
Copy Editing by Graham Paul Donovan
ISBN- 9781090582249

About the Book:

this is no longer entertainment is formed entirely out of untreated anonymous or pseudonymous text found in the open comments sections of media websites and other digital platforms. It was composed by filtering this un-authored writing through a process of immediate, instinctive selection and reframing, which is inevitably modulated by the author's interests and emotional temperature. The poem's composition roughly covers the period 2014-2017; a period marked by a range of notable social-political shifts and events.

In its use of avant-garde compositional methods as parallels with experimental documentary filmmaking practices, *this is no longer entertainment* borrows from and extends the documentary poetry tradition. It is a poetic exploration of public-private language and multiple/shifting personas enabled by digital technologies and communication, and their effect on social discourse and the broader political climate. Cumulatively, the juxtapositions of the primary material consider mutual influences and intersections between themes like (mis)-information and error, the diffusion of authority, pop/celebrity culture, identity politics, the rise of nationalism, and others.

Acknowledgements:

My thanks to the editors of the following journals and anthologies where excerpts have appeared as individual poems: *some mark made*, *Poetry Ireland Review*, *Icarus Magazine*, *CORDA*, *Paris Lit Up*, *The Pickled Body*, *Studies in Arts and Humanities (SAH) Journal*, *Free Poetry Irish Anthology*, *Wretched Strangers*, *Hotel Magazine*, *The Tangerine*.

A non-sequential 10-page selection from this book while in progress formed the text of my limited edition pamphlet *if we keep drawing cartoons* (If A Leaf Falls Press, 2016). Thanks to publisher Sam Riviere.

Thanks also to Steven Fowler, Dominic Jaeckle and Susan Tomaselli for their encouragement and support, and to Richard Brammer and Victoria Brown at Dostoyevsky Wannabe.

Special thanks to Judith, Noah and Jesse.

1.

I'm just relieved I've finally found something that
rhymes with orange

only if you're French

'Blorenge', the Welsh mountain, is another matter

having never heard her name spoken aloud I've
been calling her "soh-lan-jee" in my head

2.

In ’87 Huey Lewis & The News released *Fore!*, their most accomplished album. I think their undisputed masterpiece is ‘Hip To Be Square,’ a song so catchy most people probably don’t listen to the lyrics. But they should, because it’s not just about the pleasures of conformity, and the importance of trends, it’s also a personal statement about the band itself.

Thank you, Patrick.

Their early work was a little too new wave for my tastes, but when *Sports* came out in ’83 I think they really came into their own, commercially and artistically. The whole album has a clear, crisp sound, and a new sheen of consummate professionalism that really gives the songs a big boost. He’s been compared to Elvis Costello, but I think Huey has a far more bitter, cynical sense of humour.

That’s funny, because The News (minus Lewis) were the backing band on *My Aim Is True*.

As far as I recall, only one of the News played on *My Aim is True*.

3.

I'm not very happy with my current business card, I'm not sure who I want to kill, the designer or the printer, or perhaps both.

The world is a shit-stain. People are fucked. I'm sick of movies and books trying to preach hope. I want to see something sicker than the world I inhabit with no possibility of redemption.

Alone on a long train ride across the balkans with a deep hangover and a fever whilst smoking herbal, anyways the fella behind me asked me what I was giggling at - I turned around and showed him - he looked away quick smart.

I kind of see him as a cold blooded stylist or technician, temporarily infatuated with him at a U2 concert from the front row and mentions some nonsense about him opening up his soul or something.

This is not an exit.

Started around 6pm and finished around 5am, stayed up went to breakfast then went to bed. Woke up around 6pm, went out got drunk. Stayed out til 6am, went to breakfast - repeat.

Being a hairy subversive type, I hated the entire concept of yuppies.

Spends too much time pouring coffee and typing on a Macbook in public because they can't afford internet at home.

It was banned in Ireland but somehow a friend of mine managed to get a copy and passed it on to me.

You don't need it. Just fuck a rat, kill it, wrap it in a Harrods catalogue, then eat it.

4.

marketing has worked perhaps too well
there are ethnic Austrians living in Italy, ethnic
    Germans in Belgium and the Czech republic,
    ethnic Swedes in Finland, ethnic Celts and
    Anglosaxons living together in the UK
we over here in the US spending trillions of dollars
still passive
consuming the pornography of family, the
    pornography of Mom's apple pie, the
    pornography of sunsets
the sheer amount of bandwidth to fill
Cheese Puff or member in hand, idly masticating
engages in a diegetic re-enactment or simulation of
    the events being portrayed
the hilarity of cat burning, the excitement in a busy
    market square
when a miscreant is about to be disembowelled
confused, disappointed, and scrolling to the bottom
we can actually cause genetic mutations simply by
    watching violence
people discuss the pleasant buzz and addiction to
    getting a tattoo
the same rush of gratified ideologico-religious/
    tribal hatred when the idealised enemy is
    dispatched

carpet bombing good, beheading bad
my local ISIS store is doing a 3 for the price of 2
    deal
you also get a free bag of popcorn
Bill your like your namesake Homer
the envious, peevish Caliban to our munificent,
    hectoring, proto-liberal Prospero
this is not good journalism
extemporised riffs on beheading
why did not religion win over Marx
as an ex revolutionary socialist you ought to be
    ashamed of yourself
veering towards drugged up zombies being
    gangbanged or tricked into sex in some way
normal just-walking-down-the-street-girls paid to
    perform
most women will do that if you offer them a few
    dollars you know
you can get them free on the internets
MPs' hawkish wings clipped by the Twitter bird,
    Wall Street is occupied, Ferguson up in arms
glamour scenes never feature a female nipple
I figured I would go enjoy some violent videos on
    LiveLeak instead
I know which kind of pornography I prefer
head and fundament, perpetually absorbing one
    another, ouroboros-like

suppressed in the calculus of perceived necessity
I tried running it through Google translate, but alas
 there's no English -> English option

5.

tanks rolled through our streets smashing cars and destroying property why? being a Muslim is a choice of ideology controlled the cul de sac that led to their school pick a different one soldiers pulled random students and people from the street and lined them up on their hands and knees are a nation of immigrants broke down our door and went through our Muslim women here in America who want to integrate - lose the hijab slashing the tires watching American sports having BBQs having your kids dress up for Halloween participating in Thanksgiving some Muslims from conservative countries take their daughters "home" for this surgery which is against U.S. law a beautiful baby boy our first son was born with jaundice against murder kidnapping theft abuse child labor withholding education or medical attention from minors troops shelled the building many children were dead my 7-day-old son was among them you have to ASSIMILATE learn the language don't move into a neighborhood with only other Syrians get to know your neighbors and become a part of society and certainly don't set yourselves apart by the way 12 of us in the hatchback sedan a furniture delivery man — it was for very little pay around $15 per day the Irish were Catholic and drunks the Italians were all thieves the Swedish were dumb the Germans were beer drinking lushes who during WWI and II were under suspicion of being engaged in spying and sabotage the Japanese were a fifth column the Chinese were good enough to break their backs building railroads but not to stay the Mexicans are fine for picking crops but they are just here for the welfare the story goes my daughters would pick me up and carry me forward like Ft. Hood Boston and San Bernadino is why we oppose bringing them here living on the brink of starvation it is civil war and no reason for asylum anyway at least five in-person interviews with each and countless phone conversations and the fence to grave American welfare was another good reason to be a refugee those stories had to be consistent with interviews given by other people who knew a caseworker about an Italian immigrant family which said "not assimilated--still eating spaghetti" lived on that hope feel free to be a refugee don't assume you have a right to be in the US or a Western European country we have our own to take care

6.

if we keep drawing cartoons they'll probably give up being terrorists

if we stop drawing cartoons they'll probably stop killing people

falling plane debris and passengers

infonews, Russell brand's revolution channel, Chomsky debates

7.

Lady Liberty with a deaths head visage
crowdsourced direct democracy through
smartphones
Yes? No? Maybe? I guess no. Why?
most of them are simple people, the villagers
just young idealists empowered by social media and
otherwise completely ignorant
lucky to have access to so many cultural events, in
addition to all the great restaurants and bars
better stick to writing about chicken tikka
this tragic Ebola pandemic the rural people still see
it as
She?
our friend Ebola will shortly put an end to such
patriotic feelings
seems to have hurt your
belief in one God". He also says, "Like rain
passports outside the Western world do not let us
citizens pass any port
ask Snowden or Assange how free is the western
of course the Philippines has a radically different
historical legacy from Finland
it could produce a T34 Tank, a MIG jet or a
Sputnik
oops... Should be The Netherlands, Luxembourg

and the US...
I see Norway is top of the happiness chart.
Followed by Switzerland, Canada, Sweden and New Zealand. Followed by Denmark, Australia and Finland. Followed by The Netherlands, Finland and the US. Followed by Ireland, Iceland and Germany. Followed by Austria, the UK and Belgium. Followed by Singapore, Hong Kong and France
I am anti everything

8.

I don’t believe the writer
why didn’t he stay with many of his fellow
    countrymen
looking like a Somali I would be concerned if I
    wasn’t stopped and questioned
it’s happened to a Muslim friend of mine who also
    travels a lot in his line of work (telecoms)

I get calls where a number is displayed but when I
    call back it’s disconnected
I suggest getting rid of the beard
look at the consistency of the people who have
    blown up planes, trains, buses and cars
many blond Scandi types?

I’ll take that as sarcasm
                    ever heard of Breivik

as a blonde totally Caucasian heterosexual female with a fairly British name and a partner of similar ethnicity I have never ever been hassled by police / I have strolled through airports in a cloud of weed stink and got a wink from a security guard / they let me take a book of matches onto the plane because they were from a famous nightclub on any rational calculus I’m more at risk from bad drivers than terrorists

9.

the tabloids chose immigrants
alien backward and repressive traditions consume
welfare
none of these reasons
connected to racism xenophobia or bigotry there
are dozens ruses
instant lottery win them are asylum seekers who
are not allowed work
anyway fake ID stolen identities name expats
hardly known for language
skills and desire to integrate abroad good word play
a criminal and seeing as he was not born in this
country an immigrant
which causes cognitive dissonance
particularly certain news media for example Mail
and Express
you having a laugh and willing to put cold hard
cash down
many don't coming from the poorer parts of
Romania or Slovakia the system needs
what colours are people thinking when they
complain who
not contributed via income tax
insurance is not unlike the rise of the pre war
brown shirts the foaming rabble with logic

I sometimes like to go to the pub through a sense
of solidarity with our fellow countrymen
debate the average unemployed person could only
dream of a student
wanted to stop being Muslim since his property has
been stolen
his family and his life on one of those multi-axis
charts
and still feel entitled
3rd world basket case tired and fallacious pensioners
on the Costa del Sol speak
mother I'd like to tell you a story when human
lives are cared for
looking at their ethnicity adopt local traditions
with roofers plumbers electricians etc
cash in hand and self employed unlucky for them
it's in the text
a few women who can speak Urdu you might want
playing some kind of demented left-wing game of
Scrabble entirely anecdotal
an immigrant who has been here for 48 years
sorry
typos

10.

it opens badly, but this is deceptive
that sickly, treacly piano invaded the soundtrack
like someone dragging a fingernail on a chalkboard
IT ISN'T EVEN IN SAN FRANSISCO!!!
the writer is adrift
hundreds of anemic films
like a skin rash
someone whose entire experience of life must have
    been acquired
probably in a classroom, possibly a cloakroom
the heights of Trumpian emptiness
unashamed to display her bad handwriting
an annoying kid and his annoyed mom
both manage to escape and guess what?
not once in this does she ask money for her friend's
    house investment
the mother still dies of breast cancer
they continue to be annoying and annoyed
stuck in a room
more than a craving for a quick burger on my mind

11.

Do you feel better now? Said Leonardo da Vinci. If the creation of meaningful art began and ended with draughtsmanship then art would be The reflexive rejection of anything not instantly understandable as an aesthetic object of contemplation, .. talkies? .. rap? 8-track? .. vinyl/and, sometimes, cd? could only be topped by a feminist artist that pulled pieces of paper out of her u rite like a teenager texting hs gfriend the nude painter swinging in a harness in The Big Lebowski when a lover had me full her tampon out... the weight of it was so surprising, the way she was so trusting and open, it is still a moment that makes my heart race, my mouth taste metallic, a disembodied mannequins head, suspended from the ceiling by wire, and illuminated by flashing lights a film of an actor dressed as a mime artist, which faces the head, which issues commands via a tape recorder on a continuous loop, sited beneath the head being fed Jelly Babies and martinis in Carolee's New York apartment (the walls of which were covered in enormous pictures of her vulva) Kim Klickbait lured me the fusing of rolls of film, which creates the medium the amorphous quality of the sensuality that meanders, cuts no straight lines, is not 'hump 'em 'n run' porn and the advertising industry have taken yet another notch of our humanity and shrink-wrapped it unpleasant raw chickens and all the nasties that go with them

12.

what happened when Irish TV interviewed them
manipulative noise, designed to confuse and
misdirect
they are part of this new craze: I think they call it
'Jazz'
the Canadian Nurses' Association has nothing to do
with Pussy Riot
these punks did a very disgusting thing for those
who goes to church
for whole my life I have been scared... first by some
bear that will take me to a forest if I will not go
to bed
you will be welcomed without face or any other
control to the "Central Station" club
Nadya is the spiting image of Marks sister in peep
show
I'm with you girls
regularly watch Breaking the Set on Russia Today
most people just latch onto the sites they agree
with
leave wikipedia alone

13.

people power and dance culture kept it going
fancy mixing St Etienne with a banjo strummer
singles and liver performances
groovy
considering todays "hot air" is all about housing
some DJs spend pootling around on their laptop ffs
    comparing Pink Floyd to Meghan Trainor
kills all serendipity

I just don't get digital recordings > analogue format
    > digital playback
cd rot, mangled cassettes, corrupt downloads from
    sites no longer operating
the sleeve, the lyrics, the artwork
photography using film, chemistry and paper prints
thin, fizzy and tinny
the gatefold, the sew on patch, the poster
skins, lighter, roach and your stash
libraries, universities and radio stations
a storage problem, a dust problem, a sound pick up
    problem

easier to program a player that wouldn't let you
    pause or skip or change track order
if you just want to mix you skip the chapters you're

finding a little dry
that is really best for people without an attic

things that demographic get up to

I got a free Sharp turntable at a recycling centre.. then bought a 1999 Sony 150w amp-£50..then a pair of 1961-71 LEAK 600 speakers..again £50... records come from op-shops or a wee 2nd shop in Edinburgh..and an op-shop on Mull came up with a worthy handful.Im listening to everything from Black Sabbath to Cocteau Twins...and the pure sound has me grooving..im still naturally digital.... but vinyl has soul...[plus i got no neighbors]...

14.

feasible there is hundreds of

musicians

ideas on paper

equipment in various family members

was second nature to

various luminaries of the underground scene have been released

listen

glimpse into

allowed to have heard it a loooonnnngggg time

(wrong spelling I know)

my opinion a collection of the best stuff found

after mastering & remixing will sound shallow

the corporate line will be "listen

& honest" which is total bullshit

doodles

hated the

embryonic

just like painters constantly

15.

I'm trying to write a song called 'Quality, reliability
and value'
promote junk food, perfume and designer clothes
rolled out and successfully integrated into YouTube,
Vimeo, Daily Motion, Tidal, Spotify, Bandcamp,
Amazon Music, Google Play, Apple Music,
Pandora, Beatport, 7digital, online radio

I look at my quarterly payments I see a nice chunk
of money coming in
I get paid properly but not from the Internet

The king was proving a point to his courtiers who
tried to drown him with flattery
he was *not* omnipotent and couldn't hold back the
tide

that's ok then cos it's not stealing, it's copying

abolish copyright and patents, the whole process is
riddled
there would be no hoarding of innovation
and there's plenty of that

16.

followed by a lot of authors
they find my timeline fascinating
I am aware of some obscure books I haven't
    purchased
my new friends accept
computers exist
and following is promotion
which is of course fine
and columnists write editorials
bemoaning
how the continued reality of the novel
to engage the modern world
can question its reluctance
Twitter would like to communicate with me
and my follow count is boosted
I know
because author title is a method of relevance
the effectiveness of this advertising
#hashtag (infinite loop)

17.

People are just not intelligent enough to appreciate things like poetry. Maybe if he tried twittering his poetry or putting it on facebook, he might have more success. Poetry has been in decline all over the world for decades. People are choosing prose over verse. Plenty of stupid poetry out there. i read fiction all the time but i couldn't tell which poets won the pulitzer ever. Poetry is invisible. And poets. I've searched online and read a sampling of his poems, and frankly I don't like them. NO ONE CARES ABOUT POETS. Not now not ever. Plus as Martin Amis says, they can't drive. Maybe because poetry really isn't very important or actually that interesting. Songs without music. Writing without precision or specificity. I like poets and poetry, but expecting anyone to care is silly.

18.

trying to cook breakfast and type at same time
a classic 50s diner pile of pancakes kind of thing or
a modern cup of coffee and a cigarette
with a clear blue sky ,Californian palm trees nearby,
the blue ocean sparkling in the morning sun

just bacon , fried bread, egg, beans in a dingy
English kitchen with a dull overcast day outside
the window
makes me drift away on a lovely soft breeze

if I had a thousand mouths I'd kiss her all over, at
the same time

19.

you may be on thin ice when sending women dick
pics by text
if not
I'd put money on your theory
newspapers seem to have gone into politics and the
internet provides a free-flowing tap of

photos of black sportsmen and asian celebs cocks, as
far as I'm aware
semi-nudity that perpetuates the psychological
construct of the vagina as dangerous
Michaelanglo could not
compete with softcore directors like Russ Meyer

men as rational seems to be a commercial decision
kind of all over the place
revenge porn, fat shaming, public upskirt photos of
unsuspecting girls
someone glued half-grapefruits to their chests

the warm glow of fact free smugness
whatever
I joined a gym with totally open changing rooms

20.

A small collection of people in different constituencies, not all operating on the same site, can't get much of a thoughtful, nuanced response. Do they think everyone should be chemically castrated on their fortieth birthday? Do you think anyone over the age of 45 is not allowed to think about sex? Commentary in 40 characters doesn't reflect public opinion. A number of people displayed a far greater understanding of metre and scansion than middle aged women going hysterical for Twilight's Taylor Lautner who was like 17. How much grief did Caroline Flack get for dating Harry Styles? Call her a lech, yes, free speech is wonderful, show up a deep visceral hatred that can be inspired by someone's physical appearance.

I was mostly repulsed by 1. Men who shorten women's names 2. Men who complain via email to there wives about the lack of sex in a relationship 3. Old men who fancy a particular young woman but don't fancy her mother. Women leching after men young enough to be their son. Or men leching after men old enough to be their grandfather. Or women leching after men old enough to be their sibling. Or women leching after women and men young enough to be their daughters or sons. Creepy young girls got into a lift with someone who after a few seconds of uncomfortable silence and awkward conversation got out.

It's an illusion you're a sanctimonious young prig. A group of women including Pam Ayers think with Spinal Tap's lyrics. I prefer the classics. I'm over 40 and sometimes find teenage boys absolutely lovely. Old fans acquainted to the guy who was arrested during the Kent Naked Bike Challenge/Awareness thing because he had an erection decided to invade the dance floor and grope a number of the ushers. I think you'd ban it because you are a man.

Unless it's toilet graffiti or schoolyard banter at a family wedding it goes right over my head which is why (takes a deep breath and holds head defiantly high) I don't understand poetry at all. Nobody calls Leonard Cohen a pervert. No doubt he'll use the Bahar Mustafa defence. Only yesterday Connor made some valid rhymes concerning Caitlin Jenner's award for bravery. I read about this on twitter. Because poems are terrible I guess it's time to start screening your mail for human excrement.

21.

Whats wrong with that, its not to be taken literally and some people enjoy anal sex.

The reality is Mr Thicks cock will not be big enough to literally tear an arse in two but in reality one can only presume produce and experience thats a bit like taking a shit in reverse.

22.

congrats on learning Icelandic, I hear
immersion isn't necessarily a silver bullet for
learning
might just be the coolest place on the planet
people handing out beards and thick sweaters to all
arrivals
like a spooky baritone parallel to Bob Mould
couldnae take yer eyes off him as he wus so
magnetic. urge anybuddy tae see him
when the opportunity arises
the kind of man I'd happily cook eggy bread, bacon
and maple syrup for
must be one of the worst chat up lines ever
that's all well and good, but 'reckless sex' in
connection to HIV / AIDS
is basically negating 30 years of gay right and AIDS
activism. most of my friends
talked in interviews about the very unsafe sex
the ghost in the machine as they put some soul into
electronica
I remember them forgetting the cymbals
options are a slow reduction over a long time
(months) using liquid Paxil (easier to titrate the
dose) or a switch to Prozac which can be easier
to withdraw from

23.

the theme is : being ignored
there's a digital barrier
those who address strangers as "my friend"
enjoyed seeing Don Draper in another role
everything he writes
in a world where just looking at someone can
bring up their personal info
involves a constant steam sniffy comments fed
straight to his brain
how cruel
trapped in a supermarket with that bloody Wizzard
song playing in a loop
leading to the girl dying in the blizzard
to my mind
you've "won" and the writer lost if you spot the
twist
why would anyone accept a few vague details about
a pork pie
also who puts the toast in?
You're obsessing over the personal. Step back;
Stop following me. Thanks
Not sure how you can spin a multi-racial
relationship in a negative way
between us - it didn't start or end
it was just mixed so that it literally went on and on

24.

get ready for strip-search
I am not one for tattoo's but that would
make a really nice one
just loved those (fade out into an
LSD phantasmagorical scene)
the Stones Free in Hyde Park
joined REM onstage
for poetry written incognito in a garden
is pretty strange considering Patti Smith headlined
the Serpentine Sessions
I would like to have been told about
the child she gave up for adoption
look up the Internet punk
the answer to ennui a heady collision

mid 60's nouveau garage rock / the visceral and the
poetic / funk and roll
see In 1976 I had just left art school and was
working as an assistant in a fashion/advertising
studio in Covent Garden
hip to new developments
excited by literary junk masquerading as art
that same year an ecstatic review in the NME
referenced all my obsessions

the Symbolist poets/painters and the fin de siecle
    French demi monde
hypnotised by a grotesque androgynous mix
it was a revelation!!
how offended an Irish person could be
I loathed with a vengeance the truly awful great
    poet came as huge disappointment / worse
self reverential caricatures by my now 28yr old ex
    art student of the rock musician as tortured poet
    captures those turbulent times
although a minor masterpiece
the codified mannerism verging on parody records
    a late poetics

I would beg for my daughter and I discovered that
    I am suspect
at the age of fourteen her love touches another
rather than Just Kids it has a timeless style and pose
    I found attractive in my early twenties

25.

a record producer who worked with the Beatles
once said
that exclamation mark was a typo. it was meant to
be a question mark. even my phone is annoyed

textures intrigue me
the detritus from under my bed
given to me when I was a kid, circa 1968
playing with soldiers or dressing up
not aware of what inspiration is
but images of changed thinking
as agent provocateur, celebrator of the outrageous,
pornographer
some examples: say, Early David Lynch films
about borders (for refugees and others ;

I live near Washington, DC, where we just had 25"
of snow
the bottom of my garden is a mess. broken plant
pots, bits of foliage and a gnome in serious need
of repair
probably quite a relief if the warehouse
mysteriously burns down
an era of rejuvenated classicism will emerge from
the ruins

sonorous and Wagnerian and, God (prefeably an
Abrahamic one) forbid, nothing involving jazz,
long hair and short skirts
in addition I-Banker poster art. rather have a Farrah
Fawcett from the 70's
than quality or thought

daddy forgot to transfer the money to the account
and you have to text him about it AGAIN
someone stepped on a cat
a visionary sharp curator from the younger
generation with international credentials
isn't that something of the "it's hip to be square"
category?

26.

Philip Glass was a taxi driver, Richard Serra had a moving company

I would be as happy if I could write as well as Stevenson than if I could write as well as Joyce

I like to pontificate on art threads but the truth is I don't know much about it

the stifling and knowing sense of cynicism

the whole installation thing feels played out

Apple's '1984' TV advert during the 1984 Superbowl was directed by Ridley Scott / in the 90s they co-opted the imagery of Einstein, Lennon, Dylan, Kermit the Frog and Picasso / all of this predates social media

"street art" retains the anti-corporate aesthetic, unfortunately it has been turned into a brand of it's own

it wasn't just graffiti, it was posting artworks to random addresses or inserting drawings into library books

27.

television has been replaced by the phone
one person speaks to another in total silence
people staring at eachother when talking has two effects
overloaded with details about the person facing overexposure
leaves me with less freedom of thought

men have this horrific fear of being exposed
we need to talk about this and shed the misunderstandings

I'm a woman, so i guess none of this applies to me
I'll only show up when the money and the murder and the rap music happens
in a bikini
obviously

sometimes the news is trash
something important humanity has lost over 100 years
get good suggestions from stock trading professionals is the wise idea
these professionals are being with us always to guide us

everything is going to be even better in the future

academia is so dry
the most inventive writing is hellaciously unfun
I agree 100 percent
it was crap
after reading "Ulysses" which I also thought was
    idiotic

time to respond to your blungeonings

1. I give a fuck what he's reading 2. I'm reading Broom of The System 3. I'm interested in art 4. Because it's the best way to find new art to enjoy 5. Thank you for the advice 6. I don't mind being influenced by DFW I think he was a great artist luckily I couldn't be him even if I tried

not ashamed to say Dave got me into Love Boat
    and Baywatch
I don't see much of this type of profundity on
    YouTube

never read any of his works
after doing some online surfing I'm definitely
    going to have to check out Infinite
it is excellent

the play between theoretical physics and religion
is creating a buzz in the town where I live

I love reading butt naked as my testicles lay in a
small bag of ice water to keep me cool

you'd need to be in a Farraday cage to figure out
exactly when he mean
"avant garde literature"
even his off-the-cuff propos have footnotes

28.

Lolita outsells Pale Fire.

I don't know whether this is true or false. I'm not bothered either way.

Underground minimal techno DJs could make more money if they switched to a more commercial sort of music.

I hope you washed out your keyboard after typing that.

Personally speaking I won't read anything self-published unless recommended by someone whose taste I trust at least a little - I read a very well-reviewed ebook on Amazon (called I think The Stone Man?) or at least the first 20/30 pages; it was terrible. Genuinely terrible.

I only read novels of between 150 and 200 pages written by people from the Slovak town of Komarno.

Oh come on.

I have a full time job, I read on the bus to work.

I am from that demographic of women over a certain age who (tries to) read books.

My wife loves harlequin romances and mills & boon to, & shes black, and Jamaican.

Also, I find that my local library has a bias towards chick-lit type books.

I watched a friend write a book about historical themes that was very interesting.

Trenchtown rocks, Bob Marley told me, I knew him, did I just get cooler?

I'm sitting outside, hogging your wi-fi. Thanks for the password.

29.

the artist
the criminal
the stereotypical hard working Mexican immigrant
they think they have an audience
Kraftwerk? Just bleeps mate
a guy pushing enter on his laptop
cut and paste mish-mash wrapped in an enormous
    ego
an ugly personality
its meaningless chatter terrible footage
anti performance or something like that
All of hip hop? Not music that
move away from blatant plagiarism
Picasso was never called an asshole
John Coltrane? Just noise
Eat, Shit, Sleep, Repeat
retro,rehash,repeat,revive,revise
My Bloody Valentine? Where are the tunes?
black power symbolism and salute
there has been no sanction at all

30.

my theme song wooden my leather black jeans
so sick
number one question you asking Fuck every
question you asking
American rapper but awesome early morning
cartoon
my neighbors called 911
this guy has lost his mind
my name is jordan Belford
follow me and i will follow u it is that simple
finished i'm devoted
pitch is a little heigh but gets me going
so damn addictive
video makes me feel scared, idk
how you create your own music?
our experienced staff
perfectly matches the sickness
kind of like something you would hear from a
native
makes me think of that commercial so i hate this
four in the morning
holy shit

31.

Why oh why do we read this insignificant tosh?
Why is it strangely magnetic when I'm scrolling
down the screen?

a series of uncomfortable memories from the night
before
clean your google results by bumpng the bad stuff
off page one

philosopher for the ages
caught sight of his reflection in the back of a spoon

being truly radical
he applied the same perception to gender as he's
doing to race and class

I like to picture him clapping like a seal in the
restaurant
looks all the more ridiculous placed next to his
much-reviled trophy wife

His music is great, His wife is hot,
He's stupidly rich...But he's a bit of a cock

Thats funny and bitchy but horrible

you’re meant to write nice things

Do you have to be Picasso to have an opinion?
Should I be reading Hello magazine instead?

32.

Dorothy wants her dress back: do you honestly think the fake novel by the Internet beauty queen is better for her than television because she reads it? This is a persistent myth. This is why we see entire rainforests being chopped down to produce Top Gear books. Clearly the best way to highlight this heinous crime is to harangue young women. Naomi Campbell, Katie Price and Victoria Beckham immediately spring to mind. What about Boris? He apparently had a great deal of ghostly help in his latest book. Not all writers are JK Rowling, I don't think anyone cares if she used a ghost. For legal reasons I'm not able to talk about the specific details of my involvement with i really can't be arsed with this who cares who wrote the book? A bunch of chemists did and she put her name on the bottle. The really shocking thing is just how little she was paid. Anxiety can be overcome by meeting a lovely man (possibly musician) and going in New York palm oil production and cattle rearing, the main causes of deforestation (rainforest trees are mainly hardwood and paper is mainly made from softwood).

33.

in the last few years I have learned to play
new musical styles build electronic amplifiers read
up on world history all for free shared
by fellow Webbers

still a massive force
for good there is a danger over
time more and more people supporting
causes resulting in less and less impact

could raise the same objection to Gutenberg's printing press (used to print 'Mein Kampf' among other things) or the invention of radio (used by Goebbels among others to broadcast political propaganda) or TV / people always take something that offers power or influence and use its opportunities to further their own ends at least it is easier now for more "ordinary" people to get their message across

the idea that misogyny is significant
on the web is total cr*p in fact the web has seen
anti-racist, feminist and anti-
homophobic concepts
since forever internet
users are incredibly savvy about things

a positive effect on real life sure there's lowlife stuff
that is simply a (tidied up!) reflection of the real
world Stephen Fry compares the web to a city -
like any city it has its slums that doesn't
mean it's not great and online slums are a damn
sight better than the real

a notable effect seems to have been to contribute to
reducing crime the hypothesis being would-be
criminals are much more tied into social
values and input of society - via social media
exposure without which

to cite revenge porn as significant
problem for the internet is even more lazy it's bad
but do you
realise how small a proportion of internet porn
makes
up? the vast majority of people will
never view it?

Shakespere would have liked Linux LaTeX and modern version control software all a product of the Internet he would also have liked Internet shopping creative talents tend to be highly obsessive so anything not directly relating to the task at hand was a distraction his handwriting was terrible and stage formatting is so the drama so getting the plays into a computer would have been helpful version control and conditionals would have made it easy to correct for audience reaction and have variants according to location and theatre constraints with eCommerce he would never have to worry about food he could just order it online and have it delivered being a product of his time there was probably some wenching going on safer and more discrete if ordered off a website so I'll say he would probably have written more not less

most of the words here seem to be under-
researched

34.

what kind of person "backs up" their gmail
account?
about 7 years worth of comments from friends on
my channel page at YouTube, removed
every word and all profundity, political opinion,
love, profanity, threats, obscenity and libel
could take you on my run in a snowbound park in
Ljubljana 10 years ago / my run up the Black
Mountain in Canberra in early 1988 ditto
besides, Emirates fly direct to Dubai from Glasgow
Paisley / having to engage the horror that is
Heathrow, luggage to follow later / happened to
our youngest and her beau from NZ / arrived
Glasgow from Heathrow, no baggage
is a perfect, albeit sad example of why we should all
be scared to death
no sympathy
being a cigarette-smoker makes him look foolish
a story of his which depicted a boy raping his
younger brother
is just one sector of the arts / not meant to be
viewed on mass, like the more out there areas of
music and visual arts
whatever offends certain sections of people is
the last stand of culture / one day completely

harmless things will be banned
can be made to disappear overnight, for any reason,
or, for that matter, for (seemingly) *no reason*
only solution is to save copies in an offline
revolving door in full swing between D.C. and
Google
its name with lofty words such as 'The Democratic
Republic of...'
serious knowledge and discourse locked behind
paywalls, or, worse, walls requiring credentials

35.

white letters and black backgrounds and on
    occasion flaming backgrounds
ablaze, on a beach, late night in summer or Autumn
shadow projected on the side of a house
is about the words, innit?

that tattooist turned a four-line poem into a five-line poem and for some reason ignored the much more pleasing and well-known typography and layout of the installations / using that corny grunge-typewriter font in lower case robs most of its weight and renders it one of those 'quotes' 12-year-olds post in lieu of wisdom on Instagram

Jet flying close to the speed of God.
Gone now in a hummingbird's heartbeat.
Only the silence now of sarsens.

I remember on New Year's Eve travelling in the back of a cold dark taxi across a cold rainy Toronto to participate in a few brain storming sessions....just to see where it may go / it was a casual atmosphere, but full of electricity / 30 top professorial and scholastic 'brainiacks' from every field of academic life / we just informally talked at first, about individual interests....

these initial few meetings led to one year of weekly symposiums / enabled by TV and the upcoming computer age

I was initially invited to deliver the history of
    taxation
ended up detailing my brief career as a military
    couturier and costume designer
(costumes - the poetic detail of history)
made me realize
art has come full circle

36.

never trusted them anyway the founder

stole the algorithm from his friend stole the idea

from the Winklevoss twins connived his associate
out of shares the list

goes on acted like the old class of robber

barons and land tyrants of last century was supposed

to represent a new breed of entrepreneur that of
the internet

guru or digerati the smartest of a new generation
that had

it with the old ways pipe dreams they got lots new

pipes around these days to invoke believable dreams

37.

I don't think there's such a thing as an inherently good or bad person. There are only good and bad actions and most people tend to do both. I guess we hold very simplistic notions of good (folks we agree with) and evil (folks we don't). These simplistic notions enable us to throw around meaningless words like hero or traitor without really considering what it means. I don't think Mr Snowden's a hero, I don't think he's a villain. Indeed I don't think about him at all and I don't understand the fuss.

I don't support warrantless surveillance (except in very rare circumstances) and I'm glad this has been brought to light (with a few exceptions) but I also don't think it's extreme to stop someone at your borders who you believe is carrying sensitive information. The two aren't mutually exclusive. It gets a little murkier in that it's probably wrapped up in some degree of intimidation.

It's pretty extreme when, in order to justify detaining him, the authorities explicitly state that journalism that seeks to inform the public about government actions is terrorism if the public might react by asking the government to change its policy.

This comment was removed by a moderator because it didn't abide by our community standards. Replies may also be deleted.

38.

How do we solve the problem of embarrassing pictures from a teenage party haunting you forever? It is indeed unfortunate that these judges appear to have the last word. A lot of the legislation of the Internet being written now has a deep importance for the future. Clearly, this topic splits people into groups. The ECJ says that in Europe there are situations where personal privacy trumps freedom to publish. The US says there are none, or none which can be made judicially. One can't believe both to be true at once. It is fascinating watching the ideologies for different regions. Maybe the different philosophies will lead to segregation of services or who knows what. It's probably the defining debate of our era. The consequences of this will go well beyond removing embarrassing pictures of our youthful excesses. There will be chain reactions of censorship and self-censorship. We haven't heard the last of this.

39.

I have a device in my pocket containing the sum of all human knowledge. I use it to view pictures of cats, and start arguments w strangers. You know those horrible "revenge your ex porn sites?

Once you start regulating the Internet, it's a slippery slope. The Internet is not a man's space. Expecting women to sign off puts them at a disadvantage. I have an obviously female ID.

Can't be bothered with the "Feminazi" stuff.

The village idiot, the conspiracist, the stalker, turn off a bunch of users. Vote off those trolls.

Ah, Twitter is for the stupid, a cesspool of crazy.

40.

somebody put a sex tape of me on the internet
a 'bad girl' (substitute 'feisty', 'assertive' for a young, middle-class woman)
filmed performing 'sex acts' on 24 strangers in a Magaluf night club
and have now managed to sell it
if someone posted a sex tape of me online and I met them face to face
you sound like a violent person
Christian Bale's outrageous outburst against a lighting technician
Jeremy Clarkson and his racist comments
he sent a death threat to someone who criticized him on a Radio 1 show
um, why, um, not, um, reference, um, the, um, bandmate, um, connection, um, if, um, that, um, is, um, the, um, pertinent, um, relationship, um
I accept every word of what you've written

41.

I’m mighty glad she’s still alive
just like the rest of us; flawed as hell
if she were a man she’d be a legendary ‘bad boy’
sometimes a change of location is all it takes
it’s very flattering to London
maybe she hid on an HGV and came in through
Dover
I like Buzzcocks, but it really is trash tv
I liked Buzzcocks when Amstel was hosting

42.

a beaten wife divorcing her abusive husband and
getting a non molestation order
wasn't in the citizenship pamphlet

some sanity amongst all the
Twitter SJWs who are the movers and shakers
they disagree with with lots of disagreeable
messages
immediately above was the room where Germaine
Greer started writing "The Female Eunuch"
some sort of canvassing of opinion
that women and transwomen are different in some
ways

they call themselves "meninists"
such jewel-like language is outside time, he thinks
the brilliant genius on the NYTimes
bold, cutting, but always polite, with never a word
out of
a strong muscular athlete like Serena Williams

"just saying" is dead right
I hadn't heard of Monroe's plea
that language is fluid, the meaning of words are
defined by how they are understood

it is not a zero sum game

43.

Quoting, or paraphrasing, someone (I forget who): Go out in London. Walk into any Starbucks.

A reasonable argument.

Imagine this situation, without immigration. Thankfully we don't have any tax avoiders here.

They speak Cantonese in Hong Kong. But otherwise, well put.

44.

the photographer isn't happy with the click-bait
    headline
at the dawning of a revolution in robotics: we are
    feeling the pressures of our aging
we are very close to self-driving cars etc
after 2 laps of the city I had to pay a taxi to drive
    there and me follow

The Blue House. Now that's a pub
great parks, nice affordable housing and an
    impressive coastline
much better than bilbao, milan, paris, malmoe,
    goteborg, brussels, Barcelona
all attributes of varying usefulness, none particularly
    central to my identity

so whose to blame for Berlin?
if they're speaking directly to you in a foreign
    language surely
EU funding is a myth. They are recycling some of
    our own money back to us
Brexity logic is a mysterious thing

I once knew an unpleasant Asian woman, do you
    think I can extrapolate

who is under threat?
why do you lot use "latte" as an insult?
zero content means you've lost

I live in Würzburg, Bavaria, but I'm from Durham
personally thankful, as you should be, for the
  contribution immigrants have made
I enjoy visiting different countries to experience
  different cultures. I am certainly not racist, far
  from it, having had Polish friends, taken them to
  work, shown them around the Yorkshire Dales
  and visited them to tea
you could say you are parasitical on their labour

people vote for fascism
I'm not comfortable with anyone not like me
  syndrome
sure, I get it, ethnicity is a fuzzy concept that blurs
  on the margins
read the Wikipedia articles on Fascism and National
  Socialism before you use the words

typical of the patronising londoncentric cool kind
  of lads
I visited the public library looking for a travel guide
I had stuff to do. You really seem obsessed with
  Muslims

the idea of a Yoruba ethnic group (bringing
together Oyos, Egbas, Ekitis etc under one
umbrella) was promoted by nationalists

the Hate will get to such a point it's just
everywhere

45.

it's bloody common sense saltwater is dangerous
people drown in water, that's common sense
neither Mr nor Mrs Kurdi knew you could drown
in water?
they must have done well not to hear about
all the people drowning drowning in the
Mediterranean
they took a "shortcut" that went horribly wrong
the dad had a life jacket so obviously knew it was
dangerous
he had a Facebook page which showed a
comfortable, but not luxurious, life
he took a gamble and it failed
they were 'fleeing' Turkey, where there wasn't a war
that is not a reason for asylum, that is economic
migration
another poor judgement on his parents' part
maybe they should apply for visas just like many
other immigrants
were they planning on crossing the Atlantic?
seriously?
they would probably end up begging in the street
is the USA morally obliged to let me in ?
darned autocorrect
Hubris and Karma come to mind

there's quite a lot of it
the danger is
people fleeing war
can't judge the decisions
moral preaching
the safety of your cosy home
the stupidity
sick of it

46.

starting that process by "othering" those trying to
come

i should feel much more empathy with these
people, or at least sympathy, but their religiosity
puts me off
thrown overboard and "So what?" Save your
sympathy
'fleeing' from perfectly stable countries across the
Mediterranean towards the better life they think
they're entitled to
that looks remarkably like an invasion
boats overwhelmingly full of black Africans
the fact the journey is traumatic is also not the
responsibility of the West

BREXIT BREXIT WE WANT OUR
COUNTRY BACK blah, blah, blah
portrait of a scared nation

I will watch and be moved and then what?
let us hope the film does not pixel out the
smugglers face

47.

where will we house them
sure we can't house our own homeless

good man John, didn't take long for "what about
our own"

yeah well they should be sent to Sunni Muslim
countries
we have nothing to do with this mess

well said John
just noticed the 28 million Euro
holy mother of god, and we are sending 600
million Euro a year of aid to Africa
what about the Irish homeless
dying because of queues in cancer care
drug rehabs being shut down

this war was made by US/UK/EU globalists
we Irish are so helpful to others

U r wrong mate
them lads are brain washed by Israel and the US
Joe Biden's son is appointed as the chief of
Ukrainian gas companies

this has nothing to do with open borders
it had nothing to do with closed borders when we
accepted just 30 Jewish refugees in the 1930s

when our forefathers left these shores they had to
work

when exactly did we give "billions" to the third
word Clara?
such a caring attitude

name is Ciara
this country is sinking under the weight of mass
immigration
we take on people who should not be here
30 years ago a few people came and went mostly
from Europe
is not the same as Africa and Asia
one only needs to see the destructive results
face reality or continue making convenient glib
unrealistic

threads like this are thoroughly depressing
we'll wave a tricolour or a rainbow flag and feel
good about ourselves
in the end we're still the same mean, spiteful,
reactionary country

red thumb is on the left

48.

easy to say that because of not being Irish you are
been discriminated against
mostly Irish people are very nice
these so-called Equality Officers are biased
there is something Sinister about the Tesco's quest
for power
in one store I found a few of the workers there
bullies who were sneering slanderers
I tried to get St.Patrick's day off and was told no
because two other Polish people had it off
another case why multicultureism wil not work
here
why don't we just put a noose round Ireland's neck
and hang ourselves
sorry it happened in Sligo because it is a place I
like going to
only half a story here

49.

You should all explore your prejudices deeper. You probably haven't traveled very much, but I have. It's like the American dream only wetter. These people are very well treated here in New York, Moscow, Buenos Aires, Tokyo, Leningrad. The ridebag Irish demographic get through Immigration with extra added children's friends, the sexy consequences of immigration has a much needed boost. Someones not doing their job – I totally agree jobs should be offered to the Irish first. Not in Dublin or Galway. I studied linguistics in what was then Europe of the migrants, it's disappointing that none have any interest in going to the summer trip to bog. Why not take an Irish family who have lied and stolen their way halfway across the world happily speaking up people of various nationalities and eye and skin colour? They really need to be highlighted more. Can we deport mortifying cretins like you, stopped for driving while being black, then arrested for speaking Irish, and bring in more handsome eastern europeans? I just had a snooze. There is no delete. There is no edit. There is only eternal shame and strangers in the street pointing and whispering. Expecting new arrivals to bother their hoops is mental. You'll find them in cities, like.

50.

this is a fact no mater where you go no one has anything good to say about them.they have a reputation of being spongers .of course this sign isent a nice thing to see but our goverment keep letting them in here in their droves and someone wil get pissed off as seen

Never has more truth been spoken. Dundalk is like little Africa. Many days I walked in the rain rather then get a non-Irish taxi. Starving Ethiopians in the 1980's was it? Live Aid to feed them? Well look at the big strong Africans in Dundalk now, well able to drive a Taxi and claim dole at the same time. The young Irish have been forced to leave for Australia, and Canada. Then 3500 new Irish are given passports every year to replace them. The Irish are now the ethnic minority in our own country. Enough is enough, the Celtic Tiger is over and paddy wants his country back

I don't support ignorant action like this, but it is obvious that Irish people are realty frustrated with the continuing waves of Mass Immigration. People feel powerless-they have never been consulted about the huge demographic changes that our rulers have inflicted on the country, and the countless repercussions of these changes. We badly need a political movement on the lines of UKIP to give people the feeling that someone is listening

since the culprits are likely to be goers to this church(otherwise why would they choose this sign), I think we can safely assume that these were prods

51.

There you go again with that stuff. I think you need a break. And for those who are not Christians: we don't need explain our faith. We just need to keep it and be thankful for it. I guess I don't know the context, but the guy who's interviewing him seems really rude. He interrupts him a couple times, but mostly, he just speaks as if he was talking to a mental patient, that he had to lead to the truth. No religious group on Earth today are More persecuted than Christians. I believe that Most people are aware of what events transpired the Last time this were true. I find Bono to be quite Brave for declaring his Faith this way. I now have a New found Respect for Bono for that Bravery. And I pray God will watch over Him and His Family. Kinda weird hearing this from the man who sings he stands with Cain and makes Satanic Illuminati poses. Anybody know where the full interview can be found? From the video I was led to the RTE.ie website. However, the link to the video on that site is dead. I googled RTE and got "Ireland's National Television and Radio Broadcaster" (among other things, though this seems more likely). GOD BLESS YOU AND ALL YOUR LOBED ONES, WE NEED MORE PPL TO STAND UP FOR JESUS. NOT TO BE

AFRAID TO DO SO. THANK YOU BONO. Jesus died for our sins. Would be a shame not to sin as much as possible otherwise his death would have been in vain. maybe this will shut up some of these militant atheists

52.

having unorthodox sexual intercourse is a different
    issue from
consent to a relationship of course
unimaginable vistas open up

it has never been illegal to fall in love with another
this applies likewise to watching a play about raping
    animals
some males dislike sex with other humans with
    fetishes like lavatories or wellington boots

bestiaphobia is the next new word for insertion
the owner in using the word
has already taken rights

as distinct from the zoophiles' concept of bestialists
but doesn't the notion play into the hands of
    anthropomorphists
postmodern nihilism has no limits

loving the Oxford dictionary
they are not breaking any laws above the full
    understanding of the word
paedophiles

we make sex acts with animals and children
since consent has been a requirement in
    slaughterhouses
that's how slavery works

53.

shock in art works best when it's incidental because
the casually racist murders in Sex and Death in Sigatoka is shocking until you realise
the way we treat "animals" will also come as a shock one day when
humans are incredibly good at fooling themselves which
art that does not conform to acceptable
maximise profit from appealing to the widest
censorship has become a financial
would American Psycho
forget islam, the true threat to western liberal society is
pictures had made Fight Club
somehow it still even shocks but shock will naturally continue apes
unlike now
some commentators a lot of people learn
realised them is conformity; will kill each other for?
domination by big business instrument and lowest common denominator commercial vectors means shock is inevitable
we're reduced to the animal in the equation the main character fits all too perfectly Australia's racist history

apparently when art sets out to shock and is
    shocking to people
the status quo itself is shocking

54.

Fried chicken is especially singled out as it is seen as 'low cuisine' and has less prestige than the beef burger due to its use of a cheaper meat. It's also associated with obesity. Not being able to dance is at worst a social inconvenience and not being able to jump high just restricts you to sporting activities which don't require it. It's OK to call them bitches as long as you don't have power. I'm a vegetarian. I eat meat, but vegetarianism isn't actually about abstaining from meat consumption. Vegetarianism means being open to new experiences. If an unemployed white person screams abuse at a black person on a bus… What if it's a black businessman screaming at a white unemployed man - but the white man doesn't feel intimidated? What if it's a black gangster screaming abuse at a white cocktail waitress? What if it's a Mexican cocktail waitress screaming abuse at an Italian painter, whilst an Asian baker looks on in disdain? If a black man is walking down the street and an old white lady clutches her handbag or crosses the street… Many Indians never shop at Muslim stores unless they want to buy meat, which is not sold in Hindu stores. I have many friends belonging to different races and faiths and they tell me this. I admit it is not a part of a research.

Nicolas Anelka's quenelle salute can't possibly be anti-Semitic, since there is no significant history of black people invading, occupying, enslaving or killing Jewish people. The same reason Robin Thicke got hauled over the coals for Blurred Lines, but his collaborator T.I. (who sang the most notorious line in that whole song) seemed to get a pass.

55.

so you can walk around a gallery and stroke your
 chin at a recreation of very real abuse?
we've got to put up with it cuz freedomofspeech
 for the sake of fredomofspeech?
I've yet to be offered a clear or deliberate function
 beyond pissing people off

you really should go and Twelve Years A Slave
it's quite a good film
please don't try to ban it though

56.

freedom of speech isn't all it is cracked up to be
'customers' started to use Facebook for other things
it was quite a surprise the Arab spring
a user posts a cartoon of Mohammed the prophet
in France
is it true that many Americans think Je suis is
French for Jesus?
he did not 'invent' social media. he did not invent
the self publishing upload page. someone else
did. he just nicked the idea
a Muslim family posts pictures of their son tortured
by US soldiers
I wish my daughter could find a lovely man like
that
if the whole of humanity follow the 10
commandments with love, whatever their
religion

57.

atheism is extremely dominant homeopathic guns
and bombs contain the memory of the weapons

no radio, no TV, no dancing we are screwed
groundskeeper Willie is a fictional character written
by and voiced by Americans

58.

a bit aimless and low-budget, a bit unserious
fantastically quick at thinking on his feet
effortlessly bats away over-earnest questioning
in his own bizarre way a supplicant
can be as incoherent as hell and still make sense
all froth and manages to side-step questions like a
    seasoned ballet dancer

that's an impressive ratio of wrong to words

obviously all the bigotry and racism is bad and that
just one ginormous satire
similar to that of Marine Le Pen that is proving so
    successful in France
so too elsewhere in Europe

this is no longer entertainment

they've chickened out of the deserved cowboy
    climax by banning guns
open warehouses and give free tacos(bags of
    cement, house paint) to the needy

59.

what is the answer then? let them apply for asylum
    but the law must be the law
you cannot have a situation where IS could just sail
    into Europe
a thousand strong, its madness,
who vets these people?
all those juicy inner-city constituencies too valuable
    for liblabcon
doesn't offer any solution
he just wants art to be tougher
drill a little hole in his boat so that it finally sinks at
    the end of the Biennale
let's not bring Hopkins into this, she's best ignored
plenty of people - including our own government
    - are in effect saying "let them down"
you are by implication saying "let them drown"

another 'political' work by an artist with no experience of the plight of refugees or war vitcims, more galerists, curators and critics fiancially exploiting a serious humanitarian crisis by expressing faux empathy which doesn't involve them actually doing anything to help people

I need help. Mr.Jones is right.

it doesn't include labels nor pity
it just floats quietly
and serves to begin conversations such as this

60.

Where Norfolk meets Lincolnshire is a safe country, so you are legally obliged to extend the warm hand of British hospitality. Not just a lease like Guantanamo Bay. Because of course young men at risk of being killed by Isis or Assad or the Russians or conscripted into an army to die or kill their fellow Syrians can't possible be refugees. What sort of English is that? It really is pathetic. On a German news channel they asked some migrants how bad it would be walking to Zimbabwe. I hope our leaders appreciate the symmetry. more bombing = more refugees. This will have been superseded by the Dublin Convention, people from Cuba looking to get into Europe and mass communication. 31% of this number are arriving in the Greek Island of Lesbos monthly. And your (clearly unpleasant) point is? Cyprus is safe with a nice climate. Perfect place, but we invite you to continue the conversation

61.

oh moderator - how depressing is your job?
worshipping clumps of rock is profoundly illogical
do you seriously believe Brexit is limited to a
rejection of EU bureaucracy ?

Kurt Schwitters never got his passport
I was like, yuck, what's this stuff doing in wild
cosmopolitan and outward looking Selfridges?

I read a Jeffrey Archer novel once just after I had
finished some exam studying as a wind down -
it was fucking dire
it's riddled with crime because of multiculturalism
and social cohesion is at an all time low
it goes much deeper and darker than that
no love for this country
it's all been lost through multiculturalism
exemplified perfectly by this metropolitan elite
sorry the pretentious artist deserves his abuse
- whether we name them "Britain" or "Europe" -
we need to take much more pride in our
wonderful heritage and history
as everyone knows, Britain arose from out the azure
main at heaven's command / it is in the *vicinity*
of Europe, but is entirely separated from it

I’m still supporting Europe in the Ryder Cup

62.

There's a wider conversation though, about the extent to which society values its artists. As it has always been, the people who are getting rich are not black musicians. If Prince had been born 30 years earlier he would have been a be-bopper. This is the Beatles becoming essentially a studio band after 1966. People need to write the code, design the systems etc. Why *should* musicians, authors, etc. earn vast sums of money? All e-commerce innovation happens in the porn industry. Why should anyone get paid if cavemen didn't? Why pay the plumber at all? Does Prince get paid if I flush the toilet? This comment is very lightweight. Even though I like panpipes, and also glockenspiels, I didn't have the patience to carefully read it. I used to think that talent was the magic formula, and either you had it or you didn't. In about 91 a dude at uni showed me his computer which was 'connected to computers all over the world'. Blue screen with white text on it. He was breathless with excitement. I shrugged, failed to see the point or possibility and went for lunch.

63.

I've been to Holborn tram station for an art "installation". Very interesting, I will certainly buy the book. In the late sixties/early seventies there was a shopping mall underneath Oxford Street which included a dolphinarium. It's a scandal that people are sleeping rough, of course, but if Paris can transform its ancient disused metro stations into art galleries, nightclubs, restaurants and - yes - homeless shelters, then the homeless would soon come back up and continue begging and sleeping rough! Yes, it is a dystopian nightmare. The real point is why does this stuff have to be secret? I remember buying a Russian camera from the Russian shop that was just on top of the Kings way telephone exchange. I think the Skyfall and Sherlock scenes were filmed in the disused Jubilee line station at Charing Cross. There's lots of rats down there. Plus people need UV light to stay healthy. As well as several books, television programmes, radio interiews, and multiple websites. In Berlin you can visit a cold war nuclear bunker built underneath one of the city's busiest shopping streets. It looks like they have removed the original ceramic tiles, benches etc. The river Farset from which Belfast gets its name is culverted underneath the city. The graffiti in loos? They're all fascinating, which is far more than can be said of seeing Hootie and the Blowfish live in concert. There is an urge shared by many to follow lesser-known paths, and to explore closed-off spaces. The world around us is becoming ever-more proprietary. From public space upon which we cannot 'protest' to city green space behind locked gates to this amazing underground world, we are being boxed in and made to pay whenever we want to step out of our 'productive' places and roles.

64.

watching Toxteth last night, I bet
an entry that even the entrant does not consider to
    be
the final proof
was a tough decision for the judges
a group of singers singing (like a choir)
to regenerate urban spaces with bespoke
    collaborative
enhancing communities
Donald Trump's already
visually so uninteresting, and the conceptualism is
    so tired
being told to wrap it up
by doing something worthwhile
Kim Gordon
eating a live spider in front of the tv
is just bullshit navel gazing by students high on
    Walter Benjamin
sounds really boring
wow, I guess the past 100 years just sailed past
anti celebrity and anti establishment
you ain't no artists bruv
like a flat pack furniture shop
for sale and a bookkeeper value to hang on the
    walls of the 1%

two and a half beards between them
attempting to materialise artworks which are in the
    air for free download
they're all banging each other
if Toronto is a guide
hipsters are making Dundas West really a sweet
    place
but condos are on the way
the market will find a way to monetize
Footballer wins the Nobel
subtitled How to Make Sense of All In Life By
    Repeating What Somebody Else Said About It

65.

Up there with van Gough. He "saw colours" that no one else could see. So as the schizophrenic patient is trying to escape the intrusion of the unconscious mind the surrealist makes the unconscious mind his destination. Initially I'd thought it the fancy of an endearing but pretentious young prodigy but now realise that all his work (including his odd choice of film work) bear all the hallmarks of a performance artist. Once I switched from the mundane to viewing his work via art references and language, I understood immediately what he was on about. I was part of the Beat generation myself so know your references ("bring me a coffee and a drummer") and had a latter day fine art education. By the 1990's he had a computer programme the Verbaliser to help him, as he explained about two minutes into this interview. Quite a dangerous link not just because of the risk of insanity and addiction but also psychiatric treatment. Look at the work of mainly schizophrenic patients at the Heidleberg sanitorium, now called the Prinzhorn collection. Andre Breton wrote his book Nadja, about the time he spent with Leona D a psychiatric patient. The cut ups were invented by Burroughs and Gysin. They were shown in the hut above Beckenham Junction station. The coda to 'All

The Madmen ' is 'Zane Zane Zane ouvre le chien'. But it was not just Solomon's surreal aphorisms that evoked the dream state and inspired the beat writers. While they were both inmates in the asylum William Burroughs and Brion Gysin used cut ups and the dream machine to get in touch. Antonin Artaud was put in the asylum after he returned from South America. The Seashell and the Clergyman, which influenced Un Chien Andalou One connection to surrealism David Bowie would have been aware of

66.

sardonic commentary on updating the OS on one's
iPhone
encouraged a friend of mine to study music
he drew back the curtain on his octopus in
formaldehyde
the tulips were of rare and exotic (usually virus-
infected) varieties

120 is the factorial of 5, and the sum of a twin prime pair (59 + 61). 120 is the sum of four consecutive prime numbers (23 + 29 + 31 + 37), four consecutive powers of 2 (8+16+32+64), and four consecutive powers of 3 (3 + 9 + 27 + 81). It is highly composite, superabundant, and colossally abundant number, with its 16 divisors being more than any number lower than it has, and it is also the smallest number to have exactly that many divisors. It is also a sparsely totient number. 120 is divisible by the number of primes below it, 30 in this case. However, there is no integer which has 120 as the sum of its proper divisors, making 120 an untouchable number. 120 is the atomic number of Unbinilium, an element yet to be discovered.

the building is the Readymade

I love my brick
by the way, what is a tree?
did it inspire any punks? or Pink Floyd when they
    wrote The Wall?

67.

A physical product is purely a reflection of the limitations of the prevailing historical media – becomes entirely irrelevant because the constraints that influenced its development no longer apply – now no more a thing than the airship or the twin tub – a historical aberration.

I've a few hundred vinyl albums sitting on the shelf not connecting with a PC or Mac or Portable digital device. I have mixed feelings about their predicted demise. What the Spotify effect will be, all the jazz, rock, folk, classical and other(s) composers/musicians are not going to stop writing music. It's old school: shops have exploded in Melbourne, Australia, players are seen for sale second hand. Chances are similar will happen again in a few years' time.

Junkyard is a 1982 album by Australian post-punk group The Birthday Party. The album was recorded with Tony Cohen at Armstrong's Audio Visual (A.A.V.) Studios in Melbourne in December 1981 and January 1982. Additional tracks were recorded in London's Matrix Studios with punk producer Richard Mazda in May 1982. Mazda's previous work with ATV and The Fall had brought him to their attention. Later CD re-issues added the "Release the Bats/Blast Off!" single recorded at London's Townhouse Studio with Nick Launay in April 1981. A 2nd version of Dead Joe also appears on the re-issue. Nick Cave's then-girlfriend Anita Lane co-wrote with him on two songs, "Dead Joe" and "Kiss me Black".

Thank you, Patrick.

I see "mixtape" as a hip hop word. Beyonce's album is a classic case in point. When you fall in love with one side (god forbid tell a story over 40-80 minutes) the advent of digital means it's essentially the same thing. That's a hell of a lot of extra music pulled from the pack and given the opportunity.

I have a friend who released an album on iTunes. Last year he sold five songs. This year he sold twenty. That's a 300% increase. I can't be bothered linking to the stats but vinyl sales have been trending upwards at a rate of 100%+.

Touched upon very lightly, but www.informationisbeautiful.net generously pays the artist, rather than the pockets of the likes of Pippa Middleton can be given the kind of advances I have been reading 4% and rising I imagine a modern Kate Bush would make her money from Michael Jackson's Dangerous endorsements the instantly attractive lollipop isn't necessarily

Attention span. Not many people

One day somebody will hear 'Helter Skelter' in a film soundtrack and buy it for 69p. I am not sure we will necessarily have access to "our" downloads in 50 years' time.

You're right about 1991. If Guns n Roses could do it on Appetite, then why can't Ten by Pearl Jam? I always skipped Oceans on my orange and grey battery record player on the bus.

Err, this is not very well researched.

68.

The word curate is not a synonym for "chosen" or "collected". Inverted commas are the most succinct testament for all the culture of the last 20 yrs. Obrist wrote a book, you could look ay that. Wasn't Brian Eno on the B-side? I wanted it to be good, but I got bored looking for the goodness in it. The childish optimism ofThe Fan - he who is the lifeblood of the entire enterprise; never short of obscure references, never certain entirely of what is happening. The Dead Irish Dadaists alone would be a total craich - or possibly creak. I remember hearing them on the John Peel Show, and waiting 25 minutes for the drums to kick in. Surely after this next eight...? But no. My union - the union to which I belong - still has residences of some sort to which its members can go on holiday. I don't think you're bound to accept the political nature of your holiday, it's just if you're struggling to afford your own.

69.

People are uncomfortable about their long held
beliefs being held to the light.

Well call me a microscope, call me a telescope,
call me *trompe l'œil* call me metaphor,
call me mathematics, call me projective geometry.

In the depths of WW1 some freaks looked around
and thought,
really? Are we the freaks or are they?
And hey, plus ça change.

Gurdjieff was right about not drinking twice boiled
milk.

Light is only half the story,
destruction the leitmotif of our age –
so many oppressive tropes, so little time

When Rembrandt considered us teetering on the
edge of this human pond
He didn't look up into the skies
He looked inward into his and our own eyes
The border control
The retinal role.

Intellectual framework keeps wordsmiths in work.
If you want to replace thought with a return to
craft and skills
you'll just end up with mannered art

These are modern times if ever there were.
Any dominant mode or practice becomes
mannered in the end.
Perhaps we've reached that point.

Duchamp
he is part of the mental map,
a mischief maker.
He treated art as a game

but games are what makes us human
and I was very happy
to go beyond institutionalised images.
No one satirised dry emotional gush
the way ordinary people

Some people are understandably bored by that kind
of thing.

Referendum? Very well!

So when you say the west

you imply the economic and cultural institutions
one is forced to discuss,
all cubists, surrealists, abstract expressionists, pop artists, minimalists weren't insider brands – notice how allegorical ideas are informing all kinds of music

from john cage to music concrete to post punk to 'sampling', and also quite a bit of literature (ballard, burroughs), non-mainstream theatre and dance (I can think of examples) to say nothing of modern notions of DIY interior decor, re-using and recycling junk.

Punk not junk.

Hey
I think you were replying to Buggs not me.

There is a lot of rubbish talked.
See a weird mannequin in a landscape, it's a large glass with a staircase
painted immediate experience.

Sorry that was a mis-type.

cf the rotoreliefs the stereoscopy, the nude descending a staircase, the ames room-lite of *étant données*, the

transparency of the large glass etc, the ball of string,
the standard stoppages, the wax stopper, the bicycle
wheel you are invited to spin etc.

Of course, pardon my typo.

mind distractions confused and self-referential
like saying this is an orange and holding up a pear
the reams of words are obfuscatory to the point
it doesn't really matter what was written

neither fish nor fowl anymore.

The same criticism applied to illustrated
manuscripts, cinema, photojournalism or a rebus.
It's more like saying here's some fruit.

Imagist poetry was on the go – eliot and pound, all
those allusions leading nowhere,
The Wasteland a similarly tiresome work.
But strip
its accent and character and a load of footnotes.

Some people like footnotes.

70.

a massive misfire
cheap and tacky
gimmicky and trite
literally couldn't have put less effort into it
if this is poetry then "Autotune the News" is Opera

fuck you, Mr. or Ms. Garcia
yearning for art that looks like stuff

71.

the modern age is largely about questions
you've had time to sift through the stuff that isn't
you
happy the Impressionists kept going when they
were told they were utter bullshit
Duchamp too, and his cohort
his performance in Sigur Ros' Valtari film
experiment...it's on the tube of you
doesn't work
it has been used out of context so often
but we watch them pretending to be other people
speaking other peoples words
that gives them some kind of authority
we watch them doing crazy shit on TV
we have voted them in as world leaders, we cheer
for them at sporting events, we watch their
antics on reality TV, we take their advice
and we assume
art, music are the cosy few
paid for by taxpayers

meanwhile, artists, musicians & filmmakers struggle
to make a living
why the anger?
it's easier to be snide and anonymous

we're urged to be divided along sectarian lines
to try to erode the idea of community or fraternisation
the only thing that has ever mattered is love
people who aren't rich voting for right wing parties
must know it's absolute bullshit
the loss of trade unions, the marketisation of everything, the sexualisation of children, all that stuff
also the new "disconnect from social media" trend is the new hygge and so hurrah for that
search online for a reliable source like the British Psychological Society
if not then
a ghetto vacant lot or somewhere appropriate
and in the end Jim Morrison screams about killing his father and banging his mother

About the Author:

Christodoulos Makris has published several books, pamphlets, artists' books and other poetry objects, most recently *Browsing History* (zimZalla avant objects, 2018). His book *The Architecture of Chance* (Wurm Press, 2015) was a poetry book of the year for RTÉ Arena and *3:AM Magazine*. One of Poetry Ireland's 'Rising Generation' poets, he has presented his work widely across media and borders, and has received awards, commissions and residencies from the Irish Museum of Modern Art, StAnza Festival (Scotland), European Poetry Festival, Culture Ireland, and Maynooth University among others. He is co-director of Dublin's multidisciplinary performance series Phonica, and the poetry editor of *gorse* journal and associated imprint Gorse Editions.

"one of Ireland's leading contemporary explorers of experimental poetics"
– The RTÉ Poetry Programme

"a straw in the wind, a forerunner, in Irish poetry and Irish poetry publishing"
– Harry Clifton, *The Irish Times*

"one of the finest poets, innovators and organisers in Europe"
– S. J. Fowler

Web: yesbutisitpoetry.blogspot.com
Twitter: @c_makris

40852552R00080

Printed in Poland
by Amazon Fulfillment
Poland Sp. z o.o., Wrocław